FORENSIC SCIENCE INVESTIGATOR

TAMRA B. ORR

Published in the United States of America by Cherry Lake Publishing
Ann Arbor, Michigan
www.cherrylakepublishing.com

Content Adviser: Jeffrey M. Jentzen, M.D., Ph.D., Professor, Department of Pathology, and Director, Autopsy and Forensic Services at the University of Michigan Health System
Reading Adviser: Marla Conn, ReadAbility, Inc.

Photo Credits: © Kevin L. Chesson/Shutterstock Images, cover, 1; © LukaTDB/Shutterstock Images, 5; © fstop/iStock.com, 6; © science photo/Shutterstock Images, 7; © Andreypopov | Dreamstime.com - Female Dentist Examining Jaw Xray On Computer In Clinic Photo, 8; © Johan Swanepoel/Shutterstock Images, 11; © eddiesimages/iStock.com, 12; © Olivier Le Queinec, 15; © anthonysp/iStock.com, 16; © Viktorus | Dreamstime.com - Scientist Prepares Chromatograph Oven Photo, 18; © Bogdanhoda/Thinkstock Images, 19; © Purestock/Thinkstock Images, 21; © Anthony Correia/Shutterstock.com, 22; © Shots Studio/Shutterstock Images, 24; © kali9/iStock.com, 27; © Bliznetsov/iStock.com, 28

Library of Congress Cataloging-in-Publication Data

Orr, Tamra.
  Forensic science investigator/Tamra Orr.
    pages cm.—(Cool STEAM careers)
  Includes index.
  ISBN 978-1-63362-560-0 (hardcover)—ISBN 978-1-63362-740-6 (pdf)—ISBN 978-1-63362-650-8 (pbk.)—ISBN 978-1-63362-830-4 (ebook)
  1. Forensic sciences—Juvenile literature. 2. Forensic scientists—Juvenile literature. 3. Criminal investigation—Juvenile literature. 4. Crime scenes—Juvenile literature. I. Title.

  HV8073.8.O772 2016
  363.25—dc23
                          2015005361

Cherry Lake Publishing would like to acknowledge the work of the Partnership for 21st Century Skills. Please visit www.p21.org for more information.

Printed in the United States of America
Corporate Graphics

ABOUT THE AUTHOR

Tamra Orr is a full-time writer and author living in the gorgeous Pacific Northwest. She loves her job because she learns more about the world every single day and then talks about it endlessly with her grown children (ages 24, 21, and 18). She has written more than 400 nonfiction books for people of all ages, so she never runs out of material and is sure she'd be a champion on *Jeopardy*.

TABLE OF CONTENTS

STEAM is the acronym for Science, Technology, Engineering, Arts, and Mathematics. In this book, you will read about how each of these study areas is connected to a career in forensic science investigation.

CHAPTER 1

Not Quite So Fast!

"**A**s usual, here's another complex and confusing case filled with countless pieces of evidence. And it's all wrapped up in less than an hour," Todd's dad complained, turning off the television.

"What do you mean?" Todd asked.

"Life just doesn't work that way," he explained. "There are dozens of legal and criminal shows on TV every day, and each one makes crimes look fast and simple to figure out. In real life, the police and the investigators are often working on these cases for weeks,

Forensic science investigators collect evidence from crime scenes.

months, and even years. Remember the guy we just saw who was collecting evidence and then analyzing all of it back in the lab? He was one of the **forensic scientists**. They are the connection between science and a crime."

"They sound important," Todd said.

"They are!" his dad said. "In addition to determining which evidence is relevant, they have to analyze it, document it, and often testify about it in court." He grinned. "It's probably what they do during the commercials."

Forensic pathologists and coroners both examine bodies to find out more about how the people died.

The people who study crime scene clues are known as forensic scientists. They are trained to look at the evidence and put it together like a bunch of mismatched puzzle pieces. If all goes well, when they are done, they will have a complete picture of what really happened.

Modern-day forensic scientists are all detectives, but they have several different titles and jobs. Two of these titles are forensic **pathologists** and **coroners**. A pathologist is a medical doctor who examines human remains to determine the cause of death (what killed the person—for example, knife wounds or poison) and its manner (the way it happened—for example, murder or an accident). A coroner's main duty is to hold an official inquiry, sometimes in front of a jury, into any unnatural death. Local citizens vote for the person who will be the coroner of their county.

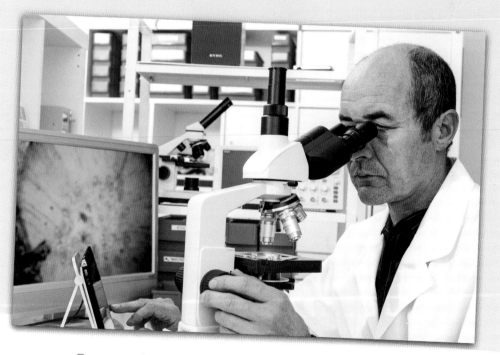

Coroners often look at tissue samples under microscopes.

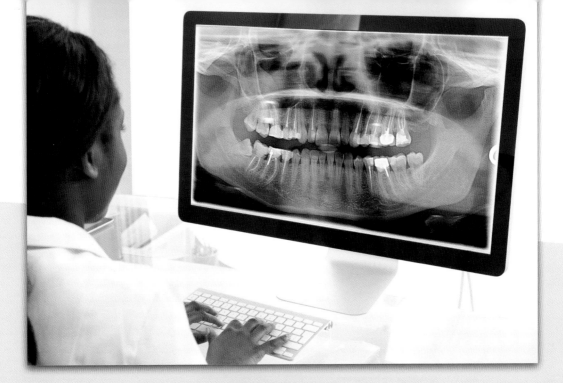

Forensic scientists may look at dental records of suspects and victims in order to identify them.

Toxicologists are another kind of forensic scientist. They specialize in testing for all kinds of chemicals, drugs, gases, and metals in a body's fluids and tissues. Some dentists are also forensic scientists. They can use bite marks or dental records to identify a body. In fact, in 1979, a forensic dentist analyzed a bite mark on a murder victim. The analysis led to the capture and conviction of serial killer Ted Bundy. He had murdered 15 people.

All forensic science specialties require many science courses as part of their training, such as biology, chemistry, anatomy, pathology, and physiology. Some of the specialties, like forensic pathology, require a medical degree or other advanced degrees. However, the choice of jobs is broad. Forensic scientists often work for the government. They may also work in private labs or in hospitals and clinics. But no matter where they work, forensic scientists spend most of their time in a lab!

THINK ABOUT SCIENCE

In addition to the specialty jobs mentioned above, forensic scientists may choose to go into:
- physical anthropology, or the analysis of skeletal remains to determine cause of death
- psychiatry or behavioral sciences, or testing for things such as mental competence
- questioned document examination, or the analysis of handwriting
- odontology, or the study of dental evidence

CHAPTER 2

ANALYZING THE EVIDENCE

Sirens scream. Police officers rush to the scene.
A murder has been committed. A victim has been
found, but . . . who is it?

How do forensic scientists identify a victim? They
may "get lucky" and find a driver's license, passport,
credit card, or other photo identification inside a wallet.
Sometimes family members are brought in to confirm
a victim's identity. Scars and tattoos can also be
good clues.

In other cases, forensic scientists have to turn to

Fingerprints are usually an accurate way to identify someone.

medical and dental records. Dental records provide details about where crowns, fillings, or missing teeth should be. Medical records might describe any tattoos, scars, birthmarks, broken bones, injuries, or surgeries a person might have had.

Of course, scientists may first check a victim's fingerprints, since each person's patterns of loops and arches aren't found on anyone else. Since 1999 the Integrated Automated Fingerprint Identification System (IAFIS) has kept more than 70 million sets of

Each piece of evidence needs to labeled.

criminal fingerprints and 34 million sets of civil prints on file. In addition, the U.S. military has millions more fingerprints of people who have served in any of the armed forces. If the victim's fingerprints have been taken, chances are he or she will be matched within a matter of hours.

The job of a forensic scientist is based on one thing: evidence. It can range from large, obvious things to tiny, even **microscopic**, things known as trace evidence. The most common things analyzed in a lab are hair, **DNA**, fingerprints, shoe prints, paint, handwriting samples, dental remains, stomach contents, and wounds. Blood stains, fibers, bodily fluids, and soil traces can contain helpful clues as well. Guns and other weapons can also be important evidence.

Forensic scientists are called on as expert witnesses to testify in court about what they have discovered. To back up their findings, they often use photographs, charts, and diagrams as well as their own detailed notes and medical reports. They keep track by putting their initials and the case number on every piece of physical evidence with which they come into contact.

THINK ABOUT TECHNOLOGY

Sometimes when a person dies, a coroner will perform a "molecular autopsy," which means running genetic tests on that person. This field is called pharmacogenomics. These tests can be done for many different things, such as if the person had a gene that might have made his or her heart suddenly stop beating, or if he or she would have reacted to a certain medicine differently than most people.

Using the Tools of the Trade

The tools forensic scientists use on a regular basis range from the very simple to the extremely complicated. One of the simpler ones is a pair of tweezers. The tweezers can pick up small pieces of glass, fiber, or other evidence. Tape is another important tool. It can be used to pick up tiny strands of hair. Other trace evidence can be collected with a vacuum cleaner that has a special filter on it. Measuring tapes are employed at a crime scene to note the distances between the victim and pieces of evidence.

UV light can help investigators find evidence that's invisible to the naked eye.

Flashlights are often used, too, but not the kind you have in the kitchen drawer. Instead, these scientists use UV, or **ultraviolet**, flashlights. This type of light can help investigators in a number of ways, including identifying counterfeit money and detecting bodily fluids at a crime scene.

Evidence bags are one of the most common tools a forensic scientist uses. These bags keep evidence from getting **contaminated** or lost. Cameras are another familiar tool that scientists use to capture clear images of the crime scene.

Investigators take photos of all the evidence they find.

Other pieces of equipment used by forensic scientists are things you have probably used in science class. For example, high-powered microscopes are used to magnify the pieces of trace evidence found at scenes. The electron microscope is especially useful. It greatly magnifies tiny pieces of evidence such as dust mites and **fungal spores**.

One of the specific instruments used by many forensic scientists is the UV visible **spectrophotometer**, a piece of equipment that can identify what chemicals a

THINK ABOUT ENGINEERING

Instead of investigating bodies, a forensic engineer analyzes materials, products, structures, and other components that did not function as they were supposed to and resulted in someone getting hurt. The forensic engineer searches for the cause of failure in order to improve the product or to provide information for court in determining the facts of an accident. For example, this type of investigator might determine if a poorly made auto part caused a serious accident to occur.

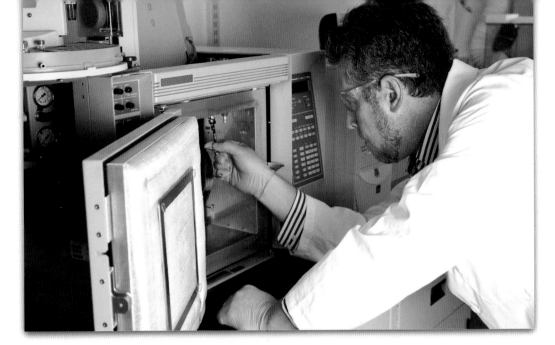

A chromatograph analyzes the specific chemicals found in different objects.

sample contains. Another useful piece of equipment is the **chromatograph**. It analyzes the different chemicals found in samples and can even identify a certain brand of cigarette smoke, coffee, ink, lipstick, or gasoline. However, all these tools are very expensive. Sometimes smaller labs send their samples to larger, better-equipped labs for analysis.

For the scientist who also works in the **autopsy** department, common tools include medical equipment such as a microscope, forceps, scalpels, bone saws, rib cutters, and scissors.

Microscopes are used to examine the tiniest pieces of evidence.

CHAPTER 4

RESPONDING TO DISASTER

Forensic scientists have to work harder than usual when large tragedies or disasters occur. These types of events have happened many times throughout history. However, some of the largest have occurred since the year 2000.

When there is a large disaster involving many people, the task for forensic scientists is huge. They must put together all the clues, help identify the bodies, and determine when and how the victims died. Examples of recent events like this include the attacks on 9/11, the earthquake and tsunami in Indonesia, and flooding from Hurricane Katrina. Forensic scientists were overwhelmed with the need to identify victims as quickly as possible. DNA was usually their best method, but it is easily damaged by heat and humidity—both of which were present in these events.

When investigating disasters with many fatalities, forensic scientists are up against some difficult challenges.

At one site of the 9/11 attacks, seen here, investigators collected remains for almost a year after the event.

Even though the 9/11 terrorist attacks happened in 2001, the effort to identify victims from tiny bone fragments continues today. While every effort was made to identify the nearly 3,000 victims, it simply was not possible. Some could be identified through DNA, dental records, or pieces of jewelry. In 2013, about half of the people remained unidentified. Since 9/11, forensic scientists have used the newest technology to analyze even the tiniest bone fragments in order to give the victims' families some peace.

In 2004, massive tidal waves from an earthquake struck the Sumatra shore and killed more than 200,000 people. Forensic scientists from all over the world came to Indonesia to help in the identification process. They used many methods, including DNA analysis, dental x-rays, and fingerprinting. Scientists spent years doing all they could to help families know what happened to their loved ones.

When Hurricane Katrina hit New Orleans on August 29, 2005, the Category-3 storm did about $100 billion of damage to the state of Louisiana. Levees meant

THINK ABOUT ART

Forensic investigators are often called on to use their artistic skills. They often sketch crime scenes for use in courtroom presentations. Many investigators are trained in image modification. They can age photographs to show how a person probably has changed since the picture was taken. Postmortem imaging is used to show how a victim appeared before they died. Unidentified skeletons may require facial reconstruction, with the artist using multiple markers and clay, as well as specialized computer software.

Forensic scientists often look at bone samples to identify victims.

to hold back water cracked, broke, and collapsed, flooding the city and destroying homes and businesses by the dozens.

The victims of Katrina were hard to identify, and many forensic scientists came to the scene to collect DNA samples. However, it was slow work and, in the end, the best method of identification came through dental records.

Sadly, fatal disasters will keep happening, and the need for forensic scientists will continue. It is their job to pull together the many clues, pieces of evidence, and other information to help identify victims and give their families some peace of mind.

CHAPTER 5

BECOMING A FORENSIC SCIENTIST

What qualities do you need to become a forensic science investigator? If you went by the actors you see on television, you might think a great wardrobe, good lighting, and some clever lines. In reality, it takes much more time, effort, and hard work.

First, getting good grades in science classes is important. Then, in college, you will need to earn a bachelor's degree in a science field such as chemistry, biology, or physics. If you're going into a specialty like psychiatry or anthropology, an advanced degree will be required.

Chemistry classes are a good foundation for future forensic science investigators.

Good speaking skills are also necessary since many of these types of investigators will provide court **testimony**. Keen observation skills are required, as investigation is all about paying close attention and seeing what most other people would miss. The ability to write clearly, precisely, and accurately will be needed for creating reports and other documents.

Forensic science investigators work in public and private laboratories, medical examiners' offices, police departments, and **morgues**. Some work for local or

*Forensic science investigators need to be
good at paying attention to details.*

state governments, while others work at the federal level
or even for international organizations.

While many of these investigators work the typical
40-hour workweek, others tend to work overtime out in
the field or stay "on call" for emergencies. According to
the Bureau of Labor Statistics, the median pay for
forensic science technicians is $25.41 per hour, or
$52,840 a year. (A median salary is defined as the
amount that half the workers earn more than and half
earn less than across the country.)

Being a forensic science investigator means picking up puzzle pieces, analyzing and examining each one, and putting them together so that they form a picture. The job takes a strong background in the sciences, keen observation skills, and attention to detail. And it takes a great deal of patience—because there is no doubt: Crimes take longer than an hour to solve, even with lots of commercials.

THINK ABOUT MATH

Analyzing blood spatter involves more than just looking at it. It is best analyzed using math. Math principles help investigators figure out the location of the victim when he or she was bleeding, and also the type of weapons and degree of impact used. Forensic investigators typically use algebra, geometry, **probability,** and **statistics** to determine everything from the paths of bullets to the time of death.

THINK ABOUT IT

A sign at the chief medical examiner's office in New York City has a saying in Latin. In English it means, "Let conversation cease. Let laughter flee. This is the place where the dead come to aid the living." What does it mean that the dead are helping the living?

French forensic scientist Edmond Locard said, "Every contact leaves a trace." This saying is the basic idea of all forensic science today. What do you think Locard meant? Reread chapters 2 and 3 for some ideas.

A good forensic scientist always asks why, when, where, what, who, and how when studying a crime scene. A good forensic scientist also has a strong sense of curiosity. Why would curiosity be an asset in this type of career?

LEARN MORE

FURTHER READING

Bertino, Anthony J. *Forensic Science: Fundamentals & Investigations*. Mason, OH: Cengage Learning, 2008.

Miller, Connie C. *Crime Scene Investigators: Uncovering the Truth*. Mankato, MN: Capstone Press, 2008.

Mooney, Carla. *Forensics: Uncover the Science and Technology of Crime Scene Investigation*. White River Junction, VT: Nomad Press, 2013.

Murray, Elizabeth. *Forensic Identification: Putting a Name and Face on Death*. Minneapolis: 21st Century Books, 2012.

Young, Karen Romano. *Science Fair Winners: Crime Scene Science*. Washington, DC: National Geographic Society, 2009.

WEB SITES

A2Z Home's Cool: CSI for Kids
http://a2zhomeschooling.com/explore/chemistry_kids/csi_unit_study_forensics_for_kids
Try some of these projects to learn more about crime scenes.

Explain That Stuff! Forensic Science
www.explainthatstuff.com/forensicscience.html
Read some basic information about investigating a crime scene.

PBS Kids: Forensics by Kalia and Carolyn
http://pbskids.org/dragonflytv/show/forensics.html
Watch this video and try to solve a mystery.

GLOSSARY

autopsy (AW-tahp-see) an examination performed on a dead person to find the cause of death

chromatograph (kruh-MAT-uh-graf) machine used to determine chemical components

contaminated (kuhn-TAM-uh-nay-tid) something made dirty, impure, or polluted

coroners (KOR-uh-nurz) officials who investigate suspicious deaths

DNA (DEE-EN-AY) deoxyribonucleic acid, a main component of genetics

forensic scientists (for-EN-sik SYE-uhn-tists) people trained to look at and interpret evidence

fungal spores (FUHNG-uhl SPOHRZ) tiny one-celled structures in various types of fungus

microscopic (mye-kruh-SKAH-pik) something so small it can only be seen with a microscope

morgues (MORGZ) places where bodies of dead people are kept until they are released for burial

pathologists (puh-THOL-uh-jists) medical doctors who examine human remains

probability (prah-buh-BIL-i-tee) the likelihood that a particular thing will happen

spectrophotometer (spek-troh-fuh-TAH-mi-ter) machine used to measure wavelengths

statistics (stuh-TIS-tiks) facts or pieces of information taken from a study that covers a much larger quantity of information

testimony (TES-tuh-moh-nee) evidence given by a witness, usually in court

toxicologists (tok-si-KOL-uh-jists) experts who look for the presence of drugs, alcohol, and other elements in body tissues or blood

ultraviolet (uhl-truh-VYE-uh-let) a type of light that cannot be seen by the human eye

INDEX